MW01232400

For
Pauline's Eyes

For Pauline's Eyes

BEN MITCHELL

Onions Publishing

First published in the United Kingdom in 2008
by Onions Publishing

Revised edition 2021

Copyright © Ben Mitchell 2008

All rights reserved. No part of this publication may be reproduced or
transmitted in any form or by any means, electronic or mechanical
including photocopying, recording or any information storage or
retrieval system, without prior permission in writing from the
publishers.

The right of Ben Mitchell to be identified as the author of this work has
been asserted by him in accordance with the Copyright, Designs and
Patents Act 1988.

ISBN 978-0-9558670-1-9

Produced by The Choir Press

Contents

My mother passed away in 2007 after over 40 years with serious kidney problems. Our parents and particularly our mothers are very special people and I feel, play a very important part in our lives. Pauline Margeret Mitchell gave me and my 3 brothers and 3 sisters everything she could and then so much more.

I had my palm read many years ago and was told that I was living the life my mother never had. I feel there might have been some truth in that. In her list of priorities my old mum never ever figured – we can never repay her for what she did for us.

I've always written poetry-come-prose and songs, working all over this world of ours as a carpenter, scribbling things down in a note book or on the back of a bit of timber. Life has been eventful, filled with interesting experiences and colourful people. What you will find in these pages are examples of what my travels and the life I lived, has taught me. My mother never knew I was an aspiring writer. This book is a tribute to her and a thank you. Wherever you are mum I hope you enjoy it and it might even surprise you. This book is For Pauline's Eyes.

I first self-published with The Choir Press some 13 years ago and in that period of time a lot has happened in my life, and worldwide generally speaking, no more so than in the last 18 months.

I think a lot of people have taken stock of life and reassessed their values and priorities in an unbelievable period in the history of mankind. A massive life changing thought provoking experience for us all, the clock is ticking and I feel we are more aware of our mortality than possibly we were say 2 years ago. There's an old saying I heard years ago, "I don't believe in burning the candle at both ends but I would hate to die and find out that I had half an inch left", I think we can all relate to that, I feel we have all had a big wake up call.

Write that book, paint those pictures, make that trip, make those dreams become a reality, do not die wishing, is their something missing in your life? I honestly feel we can all sing, we all have a book in us, there is far more to each of us than we allow the world to see. Ann, my partner, is not a poet or so she thinks, but she has written a number of poems in my publication, one *"Your breath on my face"* is, I feel a really beautiful poem.

I would like to thank all the staff at The Choir Press, Rachel, Adrian and Angeline for helping me to fulfil one of my many dreams.

I never met Ollie Sweeney as he spent his very brief 4 years fighting a very aggressive form of cancer, in and out of various hospitals the cancer which would, bless him, eventually take his life.

He made his mark in his short life with his family achieving miracles in an effort to raise money to send Ollie for specialist treatment to America, locally we were all aware of his predicament and offered our support aware of his incredible bravery and attitude.

His life so brief and eventful is a story in its self of short comings in our society and the battle his family fought to try and give him a future, all the let downs and heartbreaks and then ultimately time ran out on little Ollie.

I was going to donate the proceeds of the sales of my book "For Pauline Eyes" to "High Five For Ollie" his own Appeal Fund, but as I have said, circumstances have unfortunately changed.

There are a lot of little Ollies needing support and his family are actively involved with two Charities, Ameliamae Foundation and Keech Hospice, which I will be looking to offer support.

God bless little Ollie, he made his mark in his oh so brief life, "little Ollie now in Heaven".

Tom Cruise

She's pretty she's bubbly
She's far from being ugly
She's happy and she's lovely
She says that she loves me

But if she had to choose
Between me and Tom Cruise
Or a fit Brad Pitt
I'm afraid to say
To say I'd lose

Yeah she's light
Light and she's easy
Bright and she's breezy
Does things to please me
A living dream, special human being

She's pretty, she's witty
Sometimes she's, she's lippy
No trendy, trendy tattoos
Jimmy Choo shoes
No fancy, fancy clothes
No model pose

But if she had to choose
Between me and Tom Cruise
Or a fit Brad Pitt
I'm afraid to say
To say I'd lose

Yeah she's pretty
She's bubbly
She's far from being ugly
She's happy and lovely
And she says that she loves me.

Golden Souvenirs

Flower shirts, miniskirts
Long hair, denim flares
LSD set us free
Marijuana, cold war drama
But did they question our sanity?
Motown, James and Arthur Brown
Soundtracks of our yester, yesteryears
They are our memories
Our golden souvenirs

Sharon Tate, Charles Manson
Born to, born to hate.
Martin, Robert, brother John
Tell me Marvin
What's gone, what's gone wrong?
Please Marvin what's going,
What's going on?
Jimmy Hendrix, Eddie Kendricks
The soundtrack of our yester, yesteryears
These are our memories our golden souvenirs

Our football fix in '66
Sandie Shaw, Mary Quant
Cassius Clay, Rolling Stones
Marvin, Marvin Gaye
Fab Four we adore

But we are still rocking,
Clocking up the years
The soundtrack of our yester, yesteryears
These are our memories of
Our golden, golden souvenirs.

On the Way to Finsbury Park

We had all gone to a party in London one night. I had been playing football that afternoon and had a few beers afterwards, as you do. Well, by the time we got to this party, about ten o'clock, I was well on the way and feeling merry to say the least. As the night progressed, I met this young lady, we got on really well and when she decided she was going home I offered to drive her, sorry, I insisted, and wouldn't take no for an answer. She lived in Finsbury Park and I had no idea where that was. So I borrowed my mate's Triumph Herald (Dick Wesaloski, God bless him). I am now driving through the middle of the West End in Dick's car, with no lights on at two o'clock in the morning, with a girl I'd only met a few hours before, looking for Finsbury Park.

I'm sure you can imagine what happened next. I looked in the wing mirror and there's a great big police Range Rover with three big burly London policemen in it, with the blue light flashing, behind me. I pull over and get out of the car, these three burly coppers walk up to me, they have me surrounded, one either side of me with the car behind. One says to me, 'Do you realise you have no lights on?' I don't know why I did it, or what possessed me to do it, but I started talking in this really broad country accent, saying that I came up from down country and had come to the big city to see my fiancée, having known this young lady for at least three hours. I kept asking this gentleman where this old Finsbury Park was in an accent you wouldn't believe.

These policemen must have wondered what sort of idiot this girl was engaged to, one of them reached into the car, turned the lights on and in the process asked this young lady if she was my fiancée, which thank God she replied that she was. The police officer then shook his head and stated that he felt sorry for her to be engaged to some country idiot like yours truly. I then asked them, in my broadest village-idiot accent, where this Finsbury Park was, they invited me to follow them and they would show me, which they did.

Thank you, gentlemen, for a lot of things and a night I will never forget, and thank you to that young lady for that little white lie.

Oscar-winning Lies

I feel it in her lips
Hear it in her sighs
Feel it in her hips
In her thighs
Her Oscar
Oscar-winning lies
Make me happy
Make her smile
Plain to see
Plain to me
She's a wild
Wild, wild-child

I feel it in her lips
Hear it in her sighs
Feel it in her hips
In her thighs
Her Oscar
Oscar-winning lies
She's too hot
Too hot, too hot for me
She's trouble
Trouble guaranteed
Trouble with a capital
Capital T

I feel it in her lips
Hear it in her sighs
Feel it in her hips
In her thighs
Her Oscar, her Oscar
Oscar-winning lies
Do I need her love?
Like a flower
Flower needs rain
Need her love
Like a poet
A poet needs pain

I feel it in her lips
Hear it in her sighs
Feel it in her hips
In her thighs
Her Oscar, her Oscar
Oscar-winning lies
Was I naïve, naïve,
To trust and believe
That women don't lie
Like men don't cry,
Wishful thinking
I'll keep on drinking.

She Wears it Well

She walks down the street
Like it's a cat, catwalk
Every conversation is like
Like pillow, pillow talk
Got a pout and a swagger
Like a young, young Mick
Jagger
But she's no Marlene Dietrich,
No, no Coco Chanel,
But boy what she's got
She wears it, wears it well

She walks down the street
Like she is a celebrity
Take a good look
Good look at me
Every man's desire
Every man's fan, fantasy
But she ain't no Emily Pankhurst
No Bebe, Bebe Buell
But boy what she's got
She wears
She wears it well

She walks down the street
Like all your heavens
And all your hells.
But she's not Joan of Arc
She's no, no Adele
But boy, boy what she's got
She wears it
She wears it well.

Your Breath on My Face

As we lay together, our bodies entwined
Your breath on my face stirs thoughts in my mind
I've experienced love only a mother could know
To a life that I've given and my heart won't let go
It's a feeling so natural of sharing and caring
An unselfish love . . . but very demanding

As we lay together, your breath on my face
Stirs a passion inside me, a loving embrace
This love I'm feeling I'm unwilling to share
For it's selfish, demanding and very unfair
The most wonderful feeling I'd certainly die for,
My new meaning to life is the passion I've longed for

With your breath on my face, as I lay in your bed
I feel the woman inside me that I thought was dead
The touch of your body and tender caress
Stirs a sensuous emotion a warmth in my breast
This most wonderful feeling I could not replace
But the best thing of all is your breath on my face.

I Don't Want to Die in a Single Bed

I don't want to die in a single bed
with a road-runner
running around in my head
I could have been that
should have been this
spend my life living a wish

I don't want to die in a single bed
with an imposter inside, inside my head
being kept alive
when I'd rather be dead
just kept alive being force-fed
end my life in a living hell
spend my last days
an empty shell

Wills and pills,
meals on wheels
aches and pains
forgetting names
welcome to old age
yes, it's the final, final page
kindly please leave, leave the stage.

Voted for a Man

You voted for a man
Who didn't give a damn
Look you in the eye
Point and lie
Hell of an actor
With the wow factor
Boast and brag
Beat the drum
And fly the flag

But you're an armchair dictator
Front-room spectator
Been to the moon
In the comfort of your
Of your front room

You laud and applaud . . .
But the big man's
Just a sham
The big man's flawed
The big man's a fraud
Yeah they come in all,
All shapes and sizes
All kind of disguises
The biggest gob
Got the biggest, biggest job.

Hey Little Mama

Hey little mama
Get up and sing
Sing us a song
Sing some blues
It's been, been a long night
Long night on the booze

Hey little mama
Make this night
Make the night right
Let's make sweet music
All through, all through the night

Hey little mama
What do you say
A little bit of Levi, Aretha, Marvin Gaye
Hey little mama
Get up and sing us a song
Hey little mama let's get it on.

Pretty When She was Young

I bet she was pretty
Pretty when she was young
Turned some heads
Warmed some beds
Had her share
Her share of fun

I bet she smiled
Laughed, laughed a lot
But it's plain to see
It's something she's forgot
Yeah but she's still
Still pretty to me

I bet she was pretty
When she was young
Pretty as a picture
A strange kind of mixture
Yeah but it seems to me
She gave her love too easily

She ought to smile
Laugh more, more often
You know how it is
How it seems to soften

Soften that pretty face
Ease that heartache
Yeah I bet she turned some heads
Warmed some, some beds
Still pretty
Means everything to me.

Hotel Nacional de Cuba

She plays her songs
Sweet romantic melodies
To the gentle ghosts
Who, who haunt
The Hotel Nacional
With all its memories

You smoke your cigar
In Churchill's, Churchill's bar
As the music plays
And the bodies sway
As you move your feet
To the sound of rhythm
Of the salsa, salsa beat

Hotel Nacional, Nacional de Cuba
But shed no tear
For yester, yesteryear
For the divas and mobsters
And movie, movie stars
Who haunt, haunt Churchill's bar
Under the Hotel Nacional de Cuba's
Chand, chandeliers

Yes, she played her songs
And sweet romantic melodies
For the guests' requests
Now raise a glass
To the, the past
Now toast the Nacional's gentle ghosts
To all the memories
Under the Nacional de Cuba's
Chand, chandeliers.

Sunshine in My Mind

Fate played its part
Played a hand
Stole the future
Of this young, young man
But was this his destiny?
Self-pity
He says
Is not for me.

I can't run
And I can't walk
But I can smile
Think, laugh and talk
In quieter moments
I do reflect
My past I know
I must forget.

Sunshine in my heart
Sunshine in my mind
Strangers' love and friendship
I thank you sincerely
To man, mankind
Yes, the smallest things
To me mean everything

Sunshine through my windowpane
Warms my heart
Eased my pain
I looked in a window
What did I see?
The reflection of someone I didn't recognise as me
But the love of others
Parents and brothers
Has set me free

Sunshine through my windowpane
Helped me live
Warmed my heart
Eased my pain ...
Sunshine in my heart.

Old School Ties

They wear grey suits
Old school ties
But who are we to criticise
Their well-rehearsed, rehearsed lies
But even fools come in disguise
Rules made by fools
In grey suits
Supposedly wise and astute

Breaking down closed doors
Changing fools' rules
Changing fools' laws
Turn our backs
Ignore the facts
When you fight on the righteous side
It seems your hands and dreams
Are always tied
After the event it's easy to be wise ...

They wear grey suits
Old school ties
But who are we to criticise
Their well, well-rehearsed lies
But even fools come in disguise ...
Behind closed doors
They make their laws

Rules and regulations
Whispered covert conversations
Ignore our questions
Offer no explanations
Sometimes it's easier to turn your back
Believe the lies
Ignore the facts
Than confront the issues
And question why . . .
Yes, after the event it's easy to be wise!

Back Through the Years

When I look back
Back through the years
The heartache, sorrow
Joy and the tears
The laughter the pain
I'd do it all again
Again with you
We've had good times
Bad mad sad times
But the magic still shines
I'm yours, you're mine

Every moment every day
Forgive and forget
The things you never
Ever meant to say
When you were cruel, unkind
I'd turn a cheek
Lie, say I didn't mind
We've had good times
Bad mad sad times
But the magic still shines
I'm yours, you're mine

For I always knew
Your heart was tender
Your love forever true
We shared our dreams
Shared our life
With the joys of husband
Husband and wife
When I look back
Back through those years
I wouldn't change a thing
To me you still mean
Mean everything.

THE HOTEL THAT NEVER OPENED

Sometimes fact is stranger than fiction, this particular story is an example. I was working in Chalfont St Peter on some new housing developments, large houses and very nice indeed. Also working on this development was an electrician from Oxford whose name was Aiden, like yours truly a plastic, shandy Paddy. Myself and Aiden had a lot in common, both being football mad, with a lot of mutual friends associated with Oxford United Football Club, and both of us had strong Irish connections.

He told me a story about his family in Kerry, Southern Ireland, and in particular his uncle, Benny Moore, who had fishing boats sailing out of Dingle. Well, Benny was a real enterprising individual, not happy with just having a fleet of fishing boats, he decided to invest money in a run-down hotel with a view to refurbishing it. Whilst in the process of doing this, a big American walked into the hotel enquiring when it would be available to the general public, and that he would like to book the whole hotel for his film crew and actors, as they were about to start filming *Ryan's Daughter* and needed accommodation. Well, Benny Moore promptly agreed not believing his good fortune.

If you can remember, Robert Mitchum, John Mills and Sarah Miles were amongst the actors. Robert Mitchum evidently consumed vast amounts of whisky and made a real impression with the local female population, whilst also having the odd confrontation with a few of the local boys around Dingle. Anyway, to move on, the filming took some 18 months, and you can appreciate the expense involved in feeding and accommodating a large film crew and assorted film icons.

Well, every time Benny asked the big American about payment he was told not to worry, it would be all sorted out. Towards the end of filming, Benny again asked the big American about payment and was told not to worry, it would be sorted. At the end of filming, Benny again asked about payment and was told to go away and work out what was owed, which he subsequently did. Well, Benny evidently always had an eye for an opportunity and, on finalising the bill, he promptly doubled it. Taking the final bill to the big American, when he received it, he looked at it, then doubled it again. I'm sure you can appreciate this made Benny extremely happy.

That night Benny was out on the town painting it in Stars and Stripes, paying his bills to all and sundry, when he was approached by one of his suppliers with a view to buying the hotel. Benny thought it over and promptly sold the hotel to the local grocer who then closed it, with the intention of building a large grocery shop on the site. So, in fact, the hotel never really opened to the public.

Aiden told me this story with great enthusiasm and zest. Now, I've always had a habit of believing what I'm told, and had no reason to doubt my new plastic Paddy friend.

The story continues when myself and Ann, my partner, went to Ireland for Christmas. After visiting relations we decided to take some time out and do a bit of touring. I suggested Dingle, and off we went. We arrived there in mid-afternoon on New Year's Eve, I said to Ann, 'Let's go down to the harbour and see if we can see any of Benny Moore's boats.' As we strolled down the dockside, a gentleman was approaching in a brown suit with fetching matching hat. I stopped him and started relating the story that Aiden had told me about his uncle Benny Moore, the hotel, *Ryan's Daughter*, Robert Mitchum and the whole episode. During our conversation, I was looking down towards the boats unaware of the look on this gentleman's face, which Ann had noticed; a large grin was evident on his very Irish face.

When I had finished, he said, 'Everything you have said is true, as I'm Benny Moore', an incredible coincidence. I then asked him what happened to the hotel and he replied, 'It's the building right behind you.' The grocer had demolished the hotel and built this state-of-the-art general grocer's shop.

We had a very enjoyable New Year's Eve in Dingle and it seems the Moores are very well-respected and liked in Dingle.

Thanks, Aiden, one to remember.

A Madam

When she's had a drink
She's a bit of a madam
Bit of a minx
You can never tell
What she thinks

She sends me texts
About wild, erotic
Wild, erotic sex
She's picturesque in her
Drop dead gorgeous, low-cut dress
But this woman is not for me
Far too complex

Too hot to handle
Trouble guaranteed
Too hot to handle
Too hot for me
Trouble with a capital T

Lust is a four-letter
Four-letter word
Like hate and love
Her love can be shallow
But lust you can
Lust you can trust

When she's had a drink
She's a bit of a madam
Bit of a minx
You can never tell
What she does
What she thinks!

Sold His Soul

Played hard, died young
Punk is freedom
With a syringe drink shrink
Guitar and a gun
Yeah a '38 to my head
Pull the trigger
I'm out of here
I'm dead

Rosary beads and crucifix
Wasn't Kurt Cobain's
Not his fix
Train wreck personality
Peace, love and empathy
Forgive but never ever forget
Forget me
Sold his soul for the highest fee,
Sold out to MTV.

Rebel with a cause
But paid homage
To the corporate
Corporate applause
Rock stars
Rock stars don't live in cars

I hate myself I want to die
Help me, help me please
Silent deafening cry
Walked, talked looked like looked like suicide
Died before, before our eyes.
Suicide genes
With a suicide queen
Kurt Cobain
Was his fame to blame?

Forever Young

He slipped away so quietly
From the theatre of broken dreams
Better than the best
Different from the rest
To a life of strawberry creams

Blowing in the wind
Ain't no, ain't no sin
Not a bad, bad bone
In this rolling, rolling stone

Born a spirit free
Sang his songs
Wrote his poetry
But who needs
Those kind of memories

Blowing in the wind
Ain't no, ain't no sin
Not a bad, bad bone
In this rolling, rolling stone

Touched by magic
Like Bob Dylan playing
Playing on the wing

A life seeming so tragic
Being different ain't no,
Ain't no sin

Not a bad, bad bone
In this rolling, rolling stone
Blowing in the wind
Ain't no, ain't no sin

Yes he sang his songs that made us laugh
As he travelled his mercurial path
In his heart and mind always sunshine

Not a bad, bad bone
In this rolling, rolling stone
Blowing in the wind ain't no sin
No. 7 now in Heaven.

Star Quality

They say I've got this star
Star quality
But what you see is me
It comes so easily
Comes naturally
I said naturally

Let me say emphatically
This face poise and grace
It's me you see
Comes so easily
Comes naturally
I said naturally

You see I'm liberated
I'm celebrated
Not caged or frustrated
Not conceited or vain
What you see is me
Born to fame

Now let me state
State a fact
This ain't no charade
No charade or act
What you see
You see is me
Acting totally, totally naturally, I said naturally . . .

Sharp Suit

Sharp suit fancy ties
Funny patter little white lies
Fancy dandy so polite
Chocolate and roses
On your first night

Sharp suit fancy ties
Dress to impress
A woman's dream I must confess
A ready smile so well groomed
Romantic hero from Mills & Boon

Sharp suit fancy ties
Man of the world
So streetwise
He'll steal your dreams
Then steal your heart
Without a flicker of emotion
Tear them apart

Sharp suit fancy ties
The game won
He'll say his goodbyes
A heart of stone a heart of ice
Don't get too close
Is my, my advice

Sharp suit fancy ties
Heartbreakers in disguise.

Against all Odds

Against all odds
But with the gods
We made our mark
Turned a world to light
When once so dark!

We had our day
We had our say
We were strong, not wrong
Not meek or weak
But tell me why do the masses,
Masses sleep!

Against the tide
We don't run and hide
Yes against all odds
But with the gods
We stood toe to toe, with our foe
Confronted the demons that we didn't know

Through thick and thin
We gave it, we gave it everything
Never a thought of defeat
Yes humble, but not meek or weak
Defiant, the small man
Became, became a giant!

Yes against all odds!
But we were with, with the gods!

Take Me to the Edge

Take me to the edge
As close as you can
I'll prove I'm a woman
You prove you're a man

Take me to the limit
Take me, take me so high
Prove, prove to me
Heaven, heaven's no lie

Take me to a place
That I've never been
Show me things
I've never ever seen

Make me, take me
Give me memories
That I won't forget
Memories to treasure, never to regret

Yeah take me to heaven
Where angels all sing
Where love ain't no
Ain't no sin

Take me to a place
I've never been
Show me things
I've never ever seen

Take me
As I'm almost there
I don't know, don't know where
But I just don't, just don't care
Take me to heaven!

Dreams and Toys

The phone it rings unanswered
The babysitter knocks at the door
She doesn't need an argument
With the man she once adored.
She wonders what the night holds
She'll laugh and smile
For all the boys;
But still she'll be alone
Among the humdrum and noise

Will she ever learn to love again
Give love another try
Or will she just convince herself
In the end believe her own lies?

She tells herself she's independent
Can live life without a man
She's got everything she needs
And she doesn't give a damn
But behind the laughter and the smile
The heart that aches and bleeds,
She'll have just one drink
And swear she'll stay sober . . .
But she knows that she won't
With one drink too many
Life seems easier to cope

Will she ever learn to love again
Give love another try
Or will she just convince herself
In the end believe her own lies?

She meets a man who flatters her,
His lies she needs to believe
She'll satisfy the woman in her
Then regret it in the morning when he leaves.

She's just another story
Story that he'll relate
He's just another man
In time she'll learn to hate.

Will she ever learn to love again
Give love another try
Or will she just convince herself
In the end believe her own lies?

The only man she really loves
Lies asleep with his dreams and toys
She hopes and prays, that one day
He'll be different from last night's boys.

Love Letters Wrapped in Pink Ribbon

Love letters wrapped in pink ribbon
your picture, lays tattered and torn,
an old jumper all that's left,
plenty of memories and many regrets.
Everywhere I turn, everywhere I look
things that remind
keeps me sad and lonely, so lonely
torments my troubled, troubled mind.

Love letters wrapped in pink ribbon
your picture, lays tattered and torn,
an old jumper all that's left,
a lifetime of memories, many regrets.
Flowers you sent after that terrible row
I wish you were here, near me now.
Your smile, your touch the thought of you
I need you oh so very much.

Love letters wrapped in pink ribbon
your picture, lays tattered and torn,
an old jumper all that's left,
a lifetime of memories, many regrets.
It seems the dreams, we treasured
and shared, have died,
am I guilty of looking,
through fool's, fool's eyes?
A woman empty, incomplete,
I blame my foolish, foolish stupid pride.

The Saddest Song

He sang the saddest song
I ever heard
I felt his pain and suffering
In every word
The saddest thing
I've ever seen
To see a man
Lose his dream

To have a love
See it fade and die
So sad, can't lie
Hard to explain
That kind of pain
Not much to see
Brings a man
Man to his knees

He sang the saddest song
I ever heard
I felt his pain
In every word
The saddest thing
I've ever seen
See a man
Lose his dream

All his suffering
And heartache
How much pain
Must one man take?
I've felt his pain
No need to explain
Don't you see
I've felt the very same.

You do Things to Me

You do things to me
That are a mystery
I can't sleep
Eat or speak
Walk with two left, two left feet
Tongue-tied misty eyed
Waffle and stammer
Speak a strange grammar
Become humble-mumble
Stagger and stumble

You do things to me
That are a mystery
I'm meek, weak
Shake and tremble
Don't resemble
The man that's me

I look in a mirror
I don't recognise
Yeah the man I see,
You do things to me . . .
That are a mystery.

Light and Easy

I used to be so light
Light and easy
Life was simple
Bright and breezy
I was happy with
With the little things
Money wasn't everything

I used to be easy-going
The kind of person
Well worth knowing
I used to smile
Smile and laugh a lot
It seems it's something
Something I've forgot

I used to be a spirit free
Yes, I knew a man once
Once that man was me
I never had the Midas
The Midas touch
It never really meant
Meant that much

I used to be uncomplicated
Life was simple
Chains and ties I hated

I used to blow with the breeze
Lived my life, my life with ease
Now I look in the mirror
And what do I see ...

The reflection of a man who isn't me.

Born to Read, Born to Write

Every man at sometime
for his peace, peace of mind,
must give and take, love and hate,
tell the truth and lie,
learn to smile
learn to cry.

But some men born to read
some to write,
some so passive, some to fight,
some men born to give
some men born to take,
some to love
sadly, some to hate.

Every man at sometime
for his peace, peace of mind,
must give and take, love and hate
tell the truth and lie,
learn to smile
learn to cry.

But some born so meek
some men born so wild,
some behave like men
some like a child.
Some men have no heart
some no soul,
some men born so proud
sadly, some men born so cold.

Some men tell the truth
some always lie,
some men born so happy.
Sadly, sadly some men born to cry.

But all are born to die!

My Uncle Seamus

My uncle Seamus was my mum's younger brother and, to say the least, a bit of a character; always up for a laugh, ginger haired, a red-faced Irishman with a twinkle in his eye. A man with an eye for a deal and a ready laugh never far away. He was out with my uncle Packie on a bit of a session (as per normal) when they got home rather late. My auntie Marie had gone to bed knowing the obvious, when Seamus and Packie went out for a drink it could be any time or day before they reappeared. This particular night they got home late, well into the early hours, and the worse for wear. Seamus suggested to Packie that he go upstairs, climb into bed with his wife without turning the light on, he would then suddenly walk into the bedroom and accuse them both of having an affair. This is the sort of behaviour typical in Ireland, it's hard to imagine these two uncles of mine are in their 60s and 70s. Irish humour at its finest.

Well, Packie goes upstairs into the bedroom where my auntie Marie (God rest her soul) is half asleep. Packie climbs into bed, tucks up beside her and then throws his leg over her. You can imagine what she said, thinking it was Seamus, 'You know what you can do coming in this time of night', or words to that effect. The next minute Seamus bursts into the bedroom, turns the light on and roars what is his wife doing in bed with his brother, how could she do this to him. She sits bolt upright seeing Packie lying there. I don't think you could ever write a situation like that, or imagine her reaction.

Another incident involving Seamus was when he went to see my great-uncle, who was at death's door, literally. My great-auntie said to him, 'Now, Seamus, you haven't got any whisky on you.' Seamus replied, 'Of course I haven't, Auntie May', which meant of course he had. Seamus went into the bedroom with my great-uncle lying there with one foot in heaven the other in hell. He asked Seamus if he had a drop of the hard stuff, which Seamus produced from his overcoat. He gave my great-uncle a drop and he suddenly propped himself up on his elbow in the bed, another drop and he was sitting up in bed. After a few more tipples he was dancing around the bedroom singing Irish rebel songs, with my great-auntie May asking from the living room what was happening in there. He died the next day, but as Seamus said, 'At least he died happy.' Seamus, as you can imagine, is some boy.

He also had a travelling grocery shop many years ago, going around all the local farms. One day a farmer asked him, how was it the bills always seemed to get dearer the longer the year went on. He told me he showed this farmer the bill, and added it up in front of him justifying the end amount, only he never told him he also added the date onto the bill.

Seamus Hogan is a character to be sure. It's hard to believe what's fact and what's fiction in his life, but he certainly is interesting and forever humorous. When my cousins and his children first got married, particularly Seamus Junior and Sean, he used to say, 'Not an animal or child in the house, what sort of family is this? If you want me to come around and set the wife, just say so.'

Go on, Uncle Seamus!

A Catholic Kills a Protestant

A Catholic kills a Protestant
An Arab a Jew,
Blind indifference
To each other
Each other's point of view

A Hindu kills a Muslim
A black kills a white
One always wrong
The other,
The other always right

A radical fights the system
The unions the boss,
The Romans and Jews
Nailed Jesus,
They nailed him to a cross!

Wars bathed in blood
and the reasons are as clear, clear as mud
we must draw a line, a line in the sand
if not, mankind will be forever damned

It seems to me man is motivated
By greed and hatred,
And to some freedom,
Freedom is a word
Only some have heard!
You're wrong I'm right
Men will always
Find a reason to fight, always a reason to be right.

Romantic Yarns

You spin your romantic yarns
With charismatic charm
I'm spellbound in your arms
Putty in the palms
Palms of your hands

In a million dreams
Played a part
A million times
Stole a heart
With love so bright
Bright and breezy
With a love oh so easy

You weave your magic spell
With lines rehearsed so well
Every woman's, woman's dream
Brad Pitt, Valentino
James, James Dean
Sunshine in your smile
Laughter in your eyes

But are you just
Just a heartbreaker
Heartbreaker in disguise?
Yeah you spin your romantic yarns
With charismatic charm.

If I Placed Her on a Pedestal

If I placed her on a pedestal
One day I know she would fall
If I wrapped her in cotton wool
Tell me, tell me would I be a fool
Set her free let her fly
But would she fade, fade and die
Should I nurture and nourish
Help her bloom and flourish
If I placed her on a pedestal
One day I know she would fall

Like a beautiful scented rose
You tend, tend lovingly
As it blooms and grows
If I dress her in fine cotton
Fine cotton and lace
But we all need our own time
Our own, our own space
If I placed her on a pedestal
One day I know she would fall

It's the mystery of love
Consuming, compelling, no telling
Strange complex equation
No rhyme or reason
No explanation
If I placed her on a pedestal
One day I knew she would
She would fall.

Soft and Gentle

You are so soft and gentle
lay easy, easy on my mind
so gentle and tender
and oh so very kind.

You give your love without question,
not a question do you ask,
with a love so deep and meaningful,
I know this love, will last.
In your life no time or thoughts
it's not in you to deceive.
In this our love so complete
in this you do believe.

You are so soft and gentle
lay easy, easy on my mind,
so gentle and tender
and oh so very kind.

So many times in many ways
you prove your love
in what you do, what you say,
nothing is too much trouble
not a thing too much to ask
never a chore nothing a task.
All for love, in love's name
let me tell you now
I feel, I feel the very same.

Dreams do Come True

All the dreams I kept inside of me,
the times I wept inside,
when life disappointed
and hurt me!

My broken dreams
that never seem to materialise,
just brought tears, tears to my eyes
when life confused me.

I crept through life
frightened of the person
I knew was me, I wanted to be
but frightened, that life might ridicule me.

All those dreams I never dared to dream
but longed to share, and make my life, my life worthwhile.
Let life be kind for me and you
you see dreams, they do come true.

Old Men Talk

Old men talk
young men die,
wives widowed by old men's lies.
They blow that trumpet
beat that patriotic drum,
another senseless waste of life has begun.
We give our life and spill our blood
for reasons and causes,
as clear as mud.

Yes old men talk
young men die,
the debt we owe
to those men where the white crosses grow.
Beneath that mute, mute white cross
another life, life is lost
fallen heroes, heroes lie
old men talk, young men die!

Touched by Your Kindness

I'm touched by your kindness
Touched by your tenderness
No more empty, emptiness
Touched by your love
Your love for me
You're soft and gentle
You're tender, so kind
Go easy with my heart
Easy on my mind
Sweet lady, lady of mine

I'm touched by your kindness
Touched by your tenderness
No more empty, emptiness
Sweet lady of mine
I took a lifetime
A lifetime to find
A love like this
Cupid fired its magic arrow
Thank God it didn't miss

I'm touched by your kindness
Touched by your tenderness
No more empty, emptiness
I'll cherish that moment
That we first met
The magic of that moment
I'll never forget
Sweet lady, lady of mine
Our love forever
Our lifetime
Sweet lady, sweet lady of mine.

No Frills or Fuss

No frills or fuss
just you a friend,
a special bond between the two, two of us
you're someone I know,
I know I can trust.

It's the little things you don't forget
a friendship based on mutual respect.
A welcome smile
that doesn't hide, hide a thing
just real friendship that means everything.

No frills or fuss
just you a friend,
a special bond between the two, two of us
you're someone I know,
I know I can trust.

No false promise
you don't intend to honour,
you see, you know,
I'm sensitive, sometimes unsure insecure,
we're friends
like sister and brother.

A Mother's Love

A mother's emotions are deep and sincere
with a love that's unveiling year upon year
our children move on and love somebody new
and experience the life that we have been through
the two loves of my life I'd not want to lose
but if I could only have one, which one would I choose . . .

To My Family

Something has happened, I just can't explain
the dread inside me has gone, now there's no pain
I feel like a child, discovering myself
new horizons before me that have been years on the shelf
each day is so precious it's so easy to cope
with the strength you've given me, the pride and the hope

As I reflect on the passing years
my emotions run high, but now without fear
I'm free to do whatever I please
to go where I want, to flirt and to tease
I love my new life my dreams have come true
but my happiest time is when I'm with you.

When I was Young

When life was young
Life was fun
Climbing tall trees
Plasters on grazed knees
My life was a breeze
Mum's bedtime cuddles
Walking in puddles
Cuts and grazes
Pulling funny faces
How I reminisce and miss
Mum's bedtime kiss
Long hot summers
It wasn't heaven but it wasn't hell
I remember them oh so well
The innocence of youth an enchanting spell
Swings and slides
Scouts and Girl Guides

How the years, the years have flown
Life was bliss how I wish
How I miss
Mum's bedtime
Bedtime kiss
Dolls and toy guns
When we were young
Scared of the dark
Football in the park
Life was all new
Every lie was true
Life was a breeze
Cut knees climbing tall trees
I would like to know
Where did all the years
The years all go?

Give You My Heart

I give you my heart
Give all my dreams
To you
A love oh so special
A love so true
I'll give you my love
A love so worthwhile
The warmth of our love
The love in your smile
I'm never alone
When I'm loving you,
You're heaven-sent, I'm never blue

I give you my heart
Give all my dreams
To you
A love oh so special
A love so true
I'll give all the love
That I have to give
You are my reason
That I need to live
I'm never alone
When I'm loving you,
You're heaven-sent, I'm never blue

I give you my heart
Give all my dreams
To you
A love oh so special
A love so true
I give you my love
As one, you and me
A love forever
For eternity, eternity
I'm never alone when I'm loving you
You're heaven-sent, I'm never blue
Loving you, a dream come true.

Mother of Mine

She bakes her cakes
She always loves
Never hates
Washes dishes
But is her life just a chore
Secretly she wishes
Wishes for something more

She's a woman
Worth her weight
Her weight in gold
When she was born
They surely broke
They broke the mould

She bakes her cakes
Always loves
She never hates
Washes dishes
But is her life just a chore
Secretly she wishes
Wishes for something more

Mother of mine
Were we too deaf and blind
Too blind to see
The things you did
Did for us
You did for me
Yes she baked her cakes
Washed the dishes.

Grey Suits

We fought our wars
Against the French, Spanish, Germans
And the Boers
Built an empire
Like blood-thirsty vampires
Raped and pillaged
For a few to privilege.

Same old story since the time begun
Stole land with a pen
And at the end of a gun
Tell me who is right
Tell me who is wrong
Men in grey suits
The IRA or Vietcong
All the same all to blame.

Yeah we've fought righteous battles
And righteous wars
To muted stifled, muted applause,
Heard all the arguments
From the liberal bores
House of Commons
To the House of Lords.

Men died because men lied
We forgive the sins of Beijing
Just another episode in the tyrants' code
But when you fight on the righteous side
It seems to me
It seems to me your hands are always tied
They're all the same
All the same and all to blame.

Never be a Slave

So you earn a wage, scrimp, and save
from the cradle to the grave
and all the time another man's slave.
Work your fingers to the bone
buy a house to call your own,
it's dog eat dog, cat and mouse
pay through the nose for a doll's house.
Pay the mortgage, pay your tax
grow old early, die from a heart attack.
You live your life pay your dues,
is this the life, the life you choose?

It seems that dreams aren't par,
aren't par for the course,
sadly sometimes the fairy tale ends
so often in divorce.
Now be that person you want to be,
don't turn your love and life into slavery.
So scrimp and save
earn your, earn your wage,
but never, ever be another,
another man's slave.

A Day Out Golfing with the Elite

Peter Gibbs was, and still is, a good friend of mine. Pete is a number of years younger than myself and the rest of our then motley crew. A gang of lads with common interests, football, drink, girls, the usual for boys of our age. We also had similar attitudes to life and humour, always up for a laugh. Pete is, to put it mildly, stark-raving mad and also a very talented sportsman, big for his age, some seven years younger than the rest of us. We shared some great times together, all our nights out ended, somehow, in unusual circumstances. The stories are numerous and eventful, and sometimes involved the long arm of the law.

Pete signed professional terms for Watford Football Club at the age of 18, we had been playing together at Tring and Dudswell Saturday and Sunday football teams. He was a young talented, potentially top-class goalkeeper. I think that if Graham Taylor had been Watford's manager rather than Mike Keen, then Peter would have gone on to become a household name in the football world, at the very highest level. But Pete had a real mad streak in him, stark-raving mad boarding on lunacy. I'm sure he knows what I'm saying.

Anyway, whilst at Watford, Peter was invited to play in a golf open day at Sudbury Park Golf Club. It was the London Professional Footballers' Annual Golf Day and a host of London's finest attended. I was caddying for him which was rather difficult as I had a broken arm, having broken it playing football, so my right arm was in plaster. We arrived at Sudbury Park in Pete's top-of-the-range Hillman Imp (an old one) with one parking space vacant between a top-of-the-range Mercedes and a Rolls-Royce, which belonged to Jimmy Hill, TV presenter, football manager/ex-player and high-profile know-it-all. Pete had a few problems with his top-of-the- range Hillman Imp, notably the gear handle which kept coming out of its casing. He used to ride around Tring waving the gear stick out of the window, whilst also having a few problems with the accelerator cable, so he had a piece of string tied to the appropriate place in the engine and running under the bonnet to his hand in the car, which he used to pull to accelerate. British inventiveness at its finest.

Anyway, we pulled into this car park and he decided to park between this Merc and Rolls- Royce. The car-park attendants/hostesses were all these young ladies from the Sporting Club, I think it was in Tottenham Court Road, but all very nice young girls. Pete starts waving his gear stick out of the window and telling these girls that we had broken down, and would they mind giving us a push, which they then proceeded to do. We eventually parked between these two top-of-the-range cars, it looked funny to say the least. It certainly broke the ice with the girls from the Sporting Club.

Well, during the day we had a very enjoyable golf outing with all these high-profile football stars, and a real nice bunch of ladies from the Sporting Club, a nice meal with some lads from Chelsea, one who had just been in the national press for receiving stolen property, which gave the conversation an interesting slant, as you can imagine. Peter was also saying that he couldn't stand John Phillips (the then Chelsea goalkeeper) not realising he was sitting right behind him, which the other Chelsea boys knew and they kept feeding Pete ammunition, until in the end they said, 'Why don't you tell him, he's behind you.'

The grand finale was when we managed to get into the members-only bar, out of bounds, even for the then elite of the London football world. Alan Ball, Pat Jennings, Jimmy Hill amongst many more. As they would have to pass the bar on the way to the toilets, we would invariably acknowledge them, 'Hi, Al', 'All right, Pat', they would either ignore us or give us contemptuous looks, which we found very amusing. Anyway to continue the story, we got into a conversation with members of Sudbury Golf Club, one in particular a well-bred old chap with a cravat, blazer and badge, you know the type, drinking a half of bitter. He asked me if I was a footballer and how did I break my arm. I told him I was a professional golfer and had broken my arm falling down a bunker (Gibbsy found this very amusing). This chap replied 'Damn bad luck,' proceeding to ask me where I was a golf pro. I explained he would never have heard of it and, thinking on my feet, I said, 'Ashridge, near Berkhamsted.' Well, would you believe it, he was either playing me at my own game, or it was a pure coincidence, he said he played there every Tuesday and hadn't seen me there. Well, I took evasive action explaining that, it was my day off!

Pete and myself made a quick exit back to the elite, more our type of person, all said and done, a day to remember.

Chasing Moonbeams

Don't live your dreams
Through the silver screen
Ginger Rogers a dancing
A dancing queen

Live a life
A life of make-believe
Visions of what
Could, should have been

But what you see
On the silver screen
Is just a smoke
It's just a pipe,
Pipe dream

Beyonce, Monroe
Only ever one
One James, James Dean
On your silver
Silver screen

Don't spend your life
Chasing, trying to catch moonbeams
We are ordinary
They were ... *are* extraordinary.

On the Road Alone

It was hell of a wrench
To leave my park bench
No joke, being broke
Not very funny, very funny
Having no money
Under the stars, under the moon
This world's my front
My front room

No taxes to pay
No role, no role to play
Nowhere to sleep
Nothing to eat
But it's my life, my choice
Life on the street
No bottle of blue
No can of glue

Haversack on my back
I don't owe a penny
That's a fact
Times might be hard
But I'll survive
I won't starve
I wrote my own script
But I'm not, I'm not
A halfwit

It was hell of a wrench
To leave my park bench
I'll travel the byway
Live my life
My life my way
On the road alone
Like a rolling, rolling stone.

Money Your God

So what have you got
only a Ferrari and a yacht,
and a cardiac arrest to go,
to go with success.

chorus

It seems to me, strange,
seems so odd
how money can be, can be your God.

So you wheel and deal,
and legally steal,
all that nervous tension
you'll never ever draw a pension.

It seems to me, strange,
seems so odd
how money can be, can be your God.

Armani suits, Chivas Regal scotch,
BMW and a Rolex watch,
but what's it all worth
in the end, three barrows of earth.

finale

Tell me please
is the bottom line,
the bottom line
peace, peace of mind?

African Night

Around a fire we sat
And we spoke
Laughed at each other
Each other's jokes
Talked of wonders to his eyes
His bewilderment he didn't disguise
Young in years
But wise be he
This African man born so free

Born without the chains
Of our Western ways
I sat enthralled by the things
The things he did say
His faith in his God
Shone so bright
Around that fire
That African, African night

Our colours different
Our religion too
But we sat and listened
To each other
Each other's points of view
I learnt from him
And he from me
That wise African man
Born so free

Nothing more, nothing less
That they ask
It's seemed the weak and poor
He did bless
May his God give him strength
In his never-ending task
This African man born so wise
And born so free.

Love and Respect

Peace, love and respect
To every, every, everyone
But not the holy men
Whose holy books
Might as well
Be, be a gun.

Peace, love and respect
To one, one and all
It's just hard to believe
That the men of God
Can be so cruel.

Peace, love and respect
To all
To all mankind
God's land
It is Satan's, Satan's man.

Peace, love and respect
To all, all mankind
To the poor and old
How can man be so cold
How can we be so blind?

Peace, love and respect
To one, to one and all
Forgive
But don't forget
The actions of fools.

Simon's War

So few words of wisdom, so few,
shallow gestures, false words of peace
they say the cause is right,
God is with you, with you Simon
God be with you in this freedom fight.

This war we fight to liberate
they call this war, destiny, they call it fate.
No compromise, few words of wisdom,
yes shallow gestures false words of peace
in this, this war of hate.

In this fight for freedom, no wisdom,
this evil game they've played before
butchered, damned, another bloody evil war.
Different place a different name
familiar tune familiar game.

Filled with pride misguided heroes, heroes died,
yes Simon's wars have been fought before.
Men of valour, men so brave,
foolhardily to false causes
their lives, they willingly gave.

When the battle fought, the battle won
men of valour so brave
discarded lame, alone,
yes left alone to struggle on.
Simon's war has been fought before.

The rewards the same
in this, this evil bloody game,
your suffering and pain
oh so tragic.

A sorry, sad, sad situation
a damning fame,
the results of this bloody evil game,

Simon's war!

Love That's True

All I want from you
is love!
Love that's true,
So adore me, explore me
cherish,
but don't ignore me,
exalt and excite me
caress and ignite me!

All I want from you
is love!
Love that's true,
be tender, I'll surrender
no love pretender.
Don't cheat be sweet
light the fire that sleeps,
inside me.

All I want from you
is love!
Love that's true.
I don't need a love insincere,
just a thin, thin veneer,
paper thin doesn't mean a thing,
all I want from you, is a love that's true.

finale

Don't treat me badly
treat me wrong
for you, sadly,
I'll be gone.

All I want from you is a love that's true!

This World My Stage

The memories linger
when I wore a wedding ring upon my finger,
but your love was a prison, love a cage,
I'm a spirit free, what did they say?
That this world is a stage.

But we never shared, shared a dream
you saw objects
me!
Human beings.
My passion lay dormant
with all my frustrations
and all my torment.

You see I care,
I'm a woman with a dream
a woman with a heart
a burning light,
in your world sometimes, sometimes so dark.

Through all the years
and all my tears,
my passion and emotions
we're forced to sleep.
I had so much to give
a love so true, a love so deep.

But a woman needs love
like a flower needs rain,
a woman needs love
like a poet needs pain.

Not a love full, full of deceit
filled with mistrust
a love-cheat.
Tell me please, I'd like to know,
were you frightened of me?
The woman,
emotionally.

How Many Times

How many tears must one man cry
How many times must he lie.
How many times can one heart break
How much must one man, one man take.
How many dreams just fade and die,
How many times you ask why?

You give so much and so little in return
But still you give, never seem to learn,
You don't have to be blind,
Blind to see, love is nothing without respect and sincerity.

How many tears must one man cry
How many times must he lie.
How many times can one heart break
How much must one man one man take.
How many dreams just fade and die
How many times you ask, ask why?

To give so much and so little in return
But still you give, never seem to learn.
You don't have to be blind,
Blind to see, love is nothing without respect and sincerity.

Songs of Love are, are Endless

Songs of love are, are endless
full of pain, suffering, joy, tenderness,
every lovers share a song
love that's spent
tell me?
What went wrong.
Certain time, certain place
fondest of memories
that haunting embrace.

Songs of love that always remind
a love lost, a love not too kind
tender words once meant so much
not forgotten, but gone forever
that loving, caring touch.
Songs of love from yesteryear,
heart that ached, silent tear.
They say time will heal,
will heal a broken heart
would ease the pain,
but what chance have I
it's that song, that song of love again.

It Seems to Me

It seems to me, to you
love comes easy.
It seems to me, to you
love comes cheaply.
To you words have no value,
your love, no rhyme or reason,
do I choose to ignore
choose to be blind,
to your false love, your love treason!

Make no mistake
you delude yourself,
the true value of love
is give, give and take.
Now it looks like
it's your turn to cry,
someone else's turn,
turn to lie!

A Man for all Reasons

She wants a man for all reasons
a man for all, all seasons,
a man for all tasks
mend a fuse, cut the grass.

Yeah she's got men for all reasons
men for all, all seasons.
One on her arm
for his looks, wit and charm.

She's got a man for all reasons
a man for all, all seasons
a man with money
who can be serious, then funny.

Yes she wants a man for all reasons
men for all, all seasons.
One who's cute, a rebel in a suit,
a man to trust, another for lust.

She's got men for all reasons
men for all seasons,
but the one in her heart
the one in her head
is never the one, the one in her bed!

IT'S A SMALL WORLD

I had some New Zealand friends staying with me back in the 1980s; Chris White and Colin Shaw, with their then girlfriends and now wives, great people and friends for life. The All Blacks were to play the French at Rugby in Toulouse and myself and my Kiwi friends decided to go. To cut a long story short, it was a great trip to start with, but after two days the novelty had worn off, and being the only Englishman on board the bus, with the exception of a pain in the arse Northern Irishman, I was on my own, but in the company of my Kiwi friends, no problems.

After two days' hard drinking on the bus, how it never kicked off into a riot I will never know. There were a couple of extremely funny Kiwi lads on the coach, singing, telling jokes using the on-board microphone, but enough was enough, how the bus driver never threw them off God only knows. On the way back to London we got to the outskirts of the city, and one of these comedians had broken a skylight on the bus and is sitting on top of the roof, singing rugby songs as we are driving around Hyde Park.

When we got to our final port of call, every policeman in London is waiting for us and the bus driver's patience has finally been exhausted. Two young police officers then came onto the bus to arrest the comedian who had broken the skylight. Well, they were met with a load of abuse from the comedian and his motley crew. The two young police officers withdrew and then this gorilla disguised as a police inspector got on the bus. Whilst taking his hat and gloves off, he tells these comical Kiwis, in no uncertain terms, whichever way they wanted to come off the bus it could be arranged one way or another, and he would be willing accommodate them. They got the picture. Nobody on the bus was prepared to inform on the comic Kiwi who had damaged the skylight, and had turned into a real pain in the arse, so the big police gorilla promptly arrested yours truly, the comic Kiwi and the Northern Irish character.

I spent about three hours in this prison cell before being released. No matter what this Kiwi did I wasn't prepared to inform on him. I suppose I was stupid really, but what had started out as a really funny trip for the first 15 pints had unfortunately turned sour. It was a real good laugh and evidently one of the other buses on the trip had to turn back after things got out of hand. I was told later that the comical Kiwi was fined to the tune of £2,000 and asked to vacate the country, a shame it ended that way.

To carry on with the story, myself and a good friend of mine, Dave 'Chopper' Harris, were out in Australia visiting friends and generally having a good time. We had been to the Victorian Rugby Union Annual Dinner and Dance the night before, which had finished about three a.m., and we were going to fly to New Zealand from Melbourne Airport, at the ungodly hour of seven a.m., which meant we had about two hours' sleep. You can imagine the state we were in, but we had made it to the airport and were looking forward to seeing our friends in New Zealand.

We were delayed for a number of hours at Melbourne Airport and, whilst waiting, it quickly became apparent that one of our fellow passengers was in a far worse state than we were, which was certainly saying something. He looked considerably worse for wear, he kept misplacing his passport and briefcase, so myself and Chopper took him under our wing. He told us he was an accountant and had been in Melbourne on business and had met his brother, who was based there and they had been on the lash for about four days. During that period there had been a case in the papers where four Vietnamese had been killed in a gangland confrontation in a restaurant. Our new friend and his brother had gone down to the restaurant after this incident for a meal, he said that they weren't fighting over the food because it was great. There was claret all up the walls. I think you can imagine the type of Kiwi this fellow was.

He invited myself and Chopper to stay with him and his wife in Auckland, if our friends weren't there to meet us. Well, that's Kiwi hospitality for you — we had known him at least two hours. Anyway I digress, he started telling us how he had spent a couple of years in England and how he had gone down to Toulouse to see the All Blacks play and that his best friend, you've guessed it, had been locked up in London and deported for breaking a skylight on another bus, which had also gone to the same game.

Here I am, two years later, 12,000 miles away from home, talking to the best mate of the very same comic Kiwi, who I had had the pleasure of spending an eventful, sometimes hilarious weekend, and then three hours in a police cell to boot! It's a small world don't you think.

I Don't Read Papers or Magazines

I don't read papers or magazines,
stories of violence
topless page-three beauty queens.
Top-shelf pornography,
does it breed corruption, insanity, promiscuity,
are we too blind to see?
What is the future for humanity.

Armageddon they prophesise,
our media preaching sex and violence to a generation
global pollution, violent revolution.
Is there any peace or sanity,
yes what is the future for humanity?
No I don't read papers or magazines,
stories of violence
topless page-three beauty queens.
What they preach seems obscene,
or do they just reflect our times
will Armageddon be created,
by mankind!

Drunken Rage

He used to beat me
In a drunken
Drunken rage
Then when sober
Apologise
And say he'd change
Years of heartache
Tears and fears
Forgiving and forgetting
But in the cold light of day
A lifetime regretting.

Then par for the course
Would come, come the remorse
Gifts and the wining
Flowers and dining
Tell me how Cupid's love
Ends in man, man-made divorce?

All the verbal
Verbal abuse
All the excuses
The excuses he used . . .

Once we were lovers
Soulmates
Now our love has turned
Turned to hate
Cheating and lying
Forever denying . . .
My nights alone
Alone spent crying
No justifying
In no man's, no man's eyes
Your cheating and lying
Forever denying.

Mother's Advice

Now wear sensible shoes
Be careful the husband you choose
Don't talk to strangers
You meet in the street
Say no if he offers
Offers you a sweet
Look both ways
When you cross the road
You may kiss
Kiss a Prince Charming
Then he might turn
Turn into a toad
The love and advice
Advice of your mother

Has no equal love
Love like no other.

Turn Down the Lights

Turn down the lights
Turn them right down low
Draw the curtains
So this world, this world won't know
That we have found a love
A love so true
A lifetime searching
For a love
For a lover like you.

Turn down the lights
Turn them right down low
Draw the curtains
So this world won't know
If I had this world
In the palms
The palms of my hands,
You'd be my woman, I'd be your man.

Turn down the lights
Turn them right down low
Draw the curtains
So this world won't know
Yeah now that I have found you
With all my love I will surround you
With a love so sacred, a love so pure.
Of this our love
Of this love I am sure.

Just turn down the lights
Right down low
Draw those curtains
So this world, this world won't know.

I Lived in a World so Empty

I lived in a world so empty,
I had things material
but of no real value
of these, I had plenty.
Where love was in short, short supply
emotions a weakness
where no one cried,
just a trophy for a man,
a man to parade,
the right things said and done
a well-kept slave.
In a world where so many took
so few, so few gave.

I was just part of his image
of his success
the house, the car, a beautiful woman
in a designer dress.
All so cold, false and empty
was I frightened of the person
deep inside, inside of me?
Must I live a lie,
this spirit and soul once free
now chained,
must I say "I do" till the day I die?

This Lord too much,
too much to ask to live this lie,
so much to offer no plastic flower
for a man material, to devour.
I'm a woman with a life to live,
with emotions and feelings
with so much to give,
to give to a man, who will cherish
and love me,
for the woman I am.

I See Sadness in Those Eyes

I see the sadness in those eyes
a thing you can't, can't disguise,
beneath the smile
behind the laugh
searching hurting crying eyes,
they say it, say it all.
A broken dream, broken heart,
alone you cry, a love so tragic
gone forever love's warm tender magic.

Now alone with so much despair
no one to love, no one to care,
the loneliness you hide inside
the love you lost, gone forever,
memories and dreams
of times spent, spent together.
Where once was love that shone
now in those eyes
hate for the man you now despise!

God Save the Children

God save the children,
in their purity and innocence
with their fantasies and fairy tales,
but to some this world
is a living, living hell.

God save the children
with nowhere to sleep, nothing to eat,
with no shoes on their feet.
God save the children
from the stranger's sweets!

God save your children
keep them safe, safe from harm
from the perils of this world,
the paedophile's evil charm.
Yes, God save your children
who don't always smile,
God's child!

Seventeen and a Has-been

Seventeen and a has-been,
my dad's out of work
is on the dole,
little sister Susie dyed her hair pink
and is out of control.
My mates Jimmy and Billy
hang around town
life on the dole is getting them down,
they've given up hope
chances of work seem so remote,
seventeen and has-beens.

They ask why my views are so radical,
my opinions extreme,
you'd be the same
if you were seventeen, and a has-been.
They told me at school
my exams, my exams I must pass,
now I've qualified for a life on the dole
such a, such a tragic farce,
seventeen and a has-been.

Now my sister Berlinda jumped out the window,
her marriage on the rocks.
It seems life, is just a succession of shocks,
I think my mum lives in despair
I remember once, she really cared.
Seventeen and already a has-been,
I'm not really impressed
at things they say
by the things I've seen,
still always hope,
I'm only seventeen.

I am Black

I am black you are white
I am wrong
You are, you are right
I have no feelings
I have no say
I have no heart
In this my country
My country I play no part

You bring your culture
A new way of life
But, vulture,
Please spare me this strife
Before I was happy
A life so simple
Our needs were few
A life so shallow
So shallow you brought with you

I'm dressed in rags
I do not exist
But, vulture, I will persist
Because I am strong I am right
Even though I am black
And you are white
Why must I stumble
Why must I fall

When you, my white,
white brother
My mistakes in history
You surely can recall
Or is it just money
And all it entails
Enough reason
To see me,
My family, my country fail.

Ever Forget

Will love please release me
from your magic spell,
one moment heaven
next in hell.
Will love please explain,
why first so much pleasure,
then, then so much pain.

Will love please excuse me
if I play no part,
as you have abused me,
and broken my heart.
Took my dignity my, my self-respect,
questioned my sanity
how can I ever, ever forget?

Girls in the City, so Pretty

Girls in the city, so pretty,
dressed so trendy
frightened to be friendly,
see them in the streets
see them on the trains
all so pretty,
all so, all so vain.

Liberated girls in a woman's world,
wearing clothes the best money,
best money can buy.
Expensive perfume, magazine clones
can you, can you deny.

Live your life in a social whirl
domestic chores, just a bore.
City girl, in your material world,
diamonds, gold, furs and pearls
more to life than being a rich Miss.

Not a laugh or a smile,
as they pass you by
are they real do they feel,
do they laugh
do they cry.
Is your life being a rich bitch!

Be no Shaft of Sunlight on this Land

Be no shaft of sunlight on this land
where man's sins lay forever damned.
Be no birds do fly, in this foul polluted sky,
no trees do flourish, in this soil by death nourished.
No flowers bloom in this camp,
camp of death, camp of doom.

This scene unreal, a bastion to hate,
where the art of murder was perfected,
ethnic groups to death subjected.
No man, child, woman will survive
these cultures shall no longer thrive,
pictures on wooden walls
looks of death and despair, say it all.

The heads are shaved,
their eyes say we are doomed,
you stand and stare,
tell me Lord how should I feel,
is this Lord, is this real?
Be this done by Satan's hand
the tools, he used misguided man!

With walls of wire
fields of mines
discredit to man, mankind,
now this is not a monument to hate
but to learn from our past,
that this is not mankind's fate
but we must learn, before it's too late.

I Must Have Been a Fool

Life in this city where life can be cruel
survival is the one, golden rule.
Life among the people, people of the night
hooker for a habit, lady of the night,
life a never, never-ending fight.
No room for sentiment
just take what you can,
life is for living
don't give a, a damn.

Living in this city where life can be cruel
survival is the one, golden rule.
Live for today, tomorrow forget,
no time for sentiment
no time for regrets.
Questions don't ask
no one lives forever, nothing lasts,
disco music, neon lights
sad lonely situation
for us people, people of the night.

Living in the city where life can be cruel
where survival is the one, golden rule.
A trick here, hustle there
I'm young now beautiful,
when I'm old, will anyone care.
Life in this city
this habit and city so cruel,
I had stars in my eyes
I must have been, a fool.

A President so Dear

Butchered in Dallas sunshine
one, one November day
frightened of the truth
the things he did say,
but the price he paid
was too much, too much to ask,
the wrongs to right
too great a task.
Slain by the hand of an assassin man,
he died in his blood
on the chest of his wife
paying for freedom, the ultimate price.

The world was stunned
the brutality, and we grieved,
frightened to accept or to believe,
our hopes of a peaceful future
had come to an end
with the death of JFK
every, every free man's friend.
He died at the hand of a man
with hate in his heart,
a roll in history, he played his part.

But why take a man
who meant so, so much?
Every person our heart and soul he touched.
He stood for virtue and truth,
symbolising hope to a world,
to a world and its youth,
radiating warmth, love and humour
strength of God is what we saw,
a leader never seen, to this world before.

The ways of God are sometimes hard to accept
pain, suffering, tears, regret,
but one day, one day for sure,
a man will reappear
with the virtues of a president,
a president so dear.

MY UNCLE HUBIE HOGAN

Hubie Hogan was my mum's older brother. Well, one of them, as she was one of 18 and had 11 brothers and six sisters.

We used to go to Ireland every summer for the school holidays. Staying in this big old three-storey farmhouse in Tipperary, in a place called Lorrah. We stayed with my three uncles, Hubie, Martin and Keiren.

None of my three uncles were married at the time. We used to appear all the way from Berkhamsted after travelling with an escort, this could be a teacher, or a relative, having travelled in those days what seemed like days by train, boat, and bus.

It was a great adventure, the train used to pass by the bottom of our road in Dudswell, near Berkhamsted, going from Euston to Holyhead, and Mum used to stand on the bridge and wave to us as we passed by, it was like a scene from *The Railway Children*.

Life in Tipperary was always eventful, rural and basic, and it has left me with a lifelong love of Tipperary. The Irish are very parochial and fiercely proud of their county of origin. My family come from good hurling stock with cousins and great uncles having hurled for Tipperary, and with Ken Hogan and his son Brian recently having won All Ireland medals at Croke Park with Tipperary.

Uncle Hubie Hogan was a major influence on my life and sometimes I feel that I let him down in under-achieving. He had great hopes for me as I played football for a number of professional football clubs as a young man. Uncle Hubie had me earmarked to play for Ireland at the tender ages of eight, nine or ten.

Sorry, I digress, the man was a multitude of talents: poet, singer, musician, dancer, and comedian. He was a hurler for Lorrah, Tipperary referee, chairman of Tipperary Hurling. We used to go out on his tractor around the village of Rathcabin and he would be singing his own penned limericks in his wonderful tenor voice. I'm sure you can get the picture of my uncle Hubie Hogan.

One story I will relate to you is regarding an incident which occurred when I was about ten, and was rather alarming. Working on my uncle's farm I got ringworm from being around cows. Ringworm is not a problem with the correct medication. When I think back now, Uncle Hubie was well-read and totally aware of global events, but he decided to send me to this character who can only be described as a Celtic witch doctor. I went to see him on the cross bar of my uncle's push bike, with this big open sore of ringworm on my leg. Well, this Celtic witch doctor goes out in the garden, prays over the soil and comes back with 'holy mud', which he bandages around my sore leg. He assures me this holy mud will cure my ringworm, by the way this is all true. Well, thank God all this occurred towards the end of our holiday in Ireland. Getting back to England my mum could not believe what had happened, as I had a large lump of holy mud in my suitcase. She took me to the doctor, with this holy mud bandaged to my leg, and he asked me if I had been out in Africa. When I said that I had been in Ireland he couldn't believe it!

When Mum went back to Ireland sometime later, and queried the holy mud incident with Uncle Hubie, he said she had been in England too long and had lost her faith. And that the holy mud would have resolved the ringworm problem given a chance and time.

Well, yours truly could have been hopping around on one leg and the football career I never had would have been even less eventful!

Hubie Hogan was a unique man, multi-talented in so many ways. Although I have to question his expertise and knowledge in medical areas! I have met many characters in my life, all shapes and sizes and colours, but none quite like my uncle Hubie.

My uncle Martin stayed on the farm and would be described in this day and age as having learning difficulties. Well, he used to cook the meals for us, and looking back I can't imagine what he must have cooked for his young nephews and nieces from England, but we ate it and are still here to tell the story

Martin used to go down to see my uncle Seamus, who had a general convenience shop in the local village, every evening to watch TV and generally give Seamus a hard time without realising it. But Seamus was a good and kind brother, and we got used to hearing Martin pedalling back from his night out, stone-cold sober as he never had a drink, and he would be singing the Mass in Latin. You could hear him getting closer and louder the nearer he got to Hubie's farm.

You could not write it, fond memories, very basic and good, earthy times.

Tipperary left its mark on me.

Please Don't Leave Me

chorus

Please don't leave me tonight, tonight alone
just can't stand the breaking dawn
brings back so much emptiness
thoughts of you, the loneliness.
Please don't leave me, tonight alone
can't stand the pain here on my own.

Hold me close, close throughout this night
help ease the pain of the morning light,
asleep I have your love again
with the morning comes the truth
our love, our love did end.
Don't leave me tonight alone
it's hard to face my life
without your love, all on my own.

Please don't leave me tonight, tonight alone
just can't stand the breaking dawn
brings back so much emptiness
thoughts of you, the loneliness.
Please don't leave me, tonight alone
can't stand the pain here on my own.

This night I need for us to share
lay in your arms, please lie, say you care.
Come the morning light
comes the long, long lonely fight
must I learn to live without your love,
left with my memories of the things you once did say,
now just endless, long,
long lonely nights and days.

Alone a Tear Falls

Alone a tear, a tear falls
in a sea of despair, an unanswered call.
A cry for help we choose not to hear,
it's the voice of hunger, death and fear.
Sentenced to die before life begins
born poor, black, African
tell me?
Is that, that a sin.
Do we turn our backs
close our eyes,
we ignore the facts
deaf to their cries
as the helpless die!

Never Been to Rio

Never been to Rio
skied St Moritz,
played the Hollywood Bowl
wrecked a suite at The Ritz.
I haven't got a mansion
near Hampstead Heath,
dried out in Betty Ford's clinic,
buried with a guitar wreath.
Don't ride a Kawasaki
or a blood-red Ferrari car,
I'm an ordinary working man
no rock 'n' roll, megastar.

The Flame of Love

So he buys you roses, a few times a year
small reward for all those tears.
All the times he made you cry
all the shallow empty lies.
Did you pay the price for being too nice
and he treated you like a fool,
but I'll tell you now, my love,
true love is never, never that cruel.

chorus

How bittersweet love can be
sometimes pain, sometimes ecstasy
no chains to see
but still a form of, slavery.

Yes it's hard to explain
and not much to see
the kind of pain
can bring you, bring you to your knees.
But still you give
never, ever seem to learn
because deep in your heart
the flame of love will, forever burn.

How bittersweet love can be
sometimes pain, sometimes ecstasy
no chains to see
but still a form of, slavery.

How it all Begins ...

Rock and roll
takes its toll
–

I'm a self-made failure
I wanted to be a pilot
ended up a sailor
–

Places I've been
things I've seen, life just, just seems a dream
long time
just a memory
–

Held to ransom
by a man
a man so handsome
–

We've got dreams
dreams and schemes
they all involve moonbeams
–

Adored but flawed
with feet of clay
a high price for genius
too high a price to pay
–

Fairy tale
that led to hell
made in hell, know that story so well
on the road alone
like a rolling stone
–

.

Wasted lines
wasted minds
wasted times

–

Carefree
that used to be me
plain to see
it wasn't meant to be

–

Touched by your kindness
touched by your tenderness

–

The mistakes we make
when we are young
the grass always greener
life on the run

–

The love of a mother
has no equal
it's like no other

–

To fade and die
a chance forsaken
was it true love
that you denied

–

Bit of a lady
bit of a minx
hold on tight
when she has a drink

–

Cry a little
die a little
lie a little
wonder why a little
why life can be so fickle
—

All alone in a war
war zone
—

I dress for me
I'm what you see
I don't care
if you stare
—

On my arm
fell for my
legendary charm
—

But the streets no longer
littered with gold
can be cruel and dangerous
cruel and cold
—

Be single-minded
never blinded
by apathy, lethargy
or jealousy
make your life your
own
own destiny
—

Live your life on sin
and heroin
—

Wars are bathed in blood
sometimes the reasons
are as clear as mud

–

Wills and pills
meals on wheels
aches and pains
forgetting names
welcome to old age
it's the final stage
kindly leave the stage

–

Draw a line in the sand
if we don't
mankind damned

–

All the no's and rejections
all my so-called imperfections
I'd never guess
the no's are now
now yes

–

Fought wars to muted applause
heard all the arguments
from the liberal bores
House of Commons, House of Lords

–

I could have been a jockey
if I'd been shorter
a basketball player
if I'd been taller

–

Happy being a fisherman
happy being a missing man

–

Was I foolish and stupid
to believe in Cupid?

–

It's a mystery
lost in history

–

She'd look sexy
lying next to me
wishful thinking
keep on drinking

–

Raise your glass
to the past
whatever it was
it wasn't meant to last

–

Enjoy the laughter
because there's going
to be tears
it might not be today
tomorrow
or in later years

–

It's no joke being broke
not very funny
without any money

–

Men don't cry
like women don't lie

–

No trendy tattoos
no Jimmy Choo shoes

–

Don't make me tearful
fearful
smile and be cheerful
–

Everyone has a price
a diamond ring
or a bowl of rice
–

Lauded and applauded
and well-rewarded
–

Winners and losers
teetotallers and boozers
–

All shapes and sizes
all kinds of disguises
–

She's cultured and refined
with an educated mind
–

Never ever knew my place
never want to be
a nameless face
–

You looked rough
rough in the morning
you didn't give me
give me a warning
–

A man without love
is like a flower without rain
it's like Hendrix
without a guitar
without fame
–

Bold as brass
without any class

–

Honey sweet
so complete

–

Boom and bust
deceit and mistrust

–

To be a writer
you have to be a fighter

–

Ticket to the cricket
a day at Lord's
with the Barmy Army
not Nigel or Julian
in their wine-red cords ...
yeah, a ticket at the cricket
the green serene pastures of Lord's

–

He used to dance a lot
around the deck of his big yacht
then one day he forgot
fell off his great big yacht.
Please come and rescue me
from this great big sea.

–

Don't cheat
no cheap treat

–

Live your life
with memories
saddened with regret
things from your past
you would like to forget

–

In a world fresh and new
and it all belongs
belongs to you
if only that
that was true

–

You don't need a gun
to kill,
to hurt someone

–

Live your life
on the edge of a knife

–

With my voice
should be driving
a Rolls-Royce
with a guitar
could have made me
made me a star
a life of champagne
and Russian caviar

–

What is our love worth
made in Heaven
ruined on Earth

–

Heard it on the radio
must be more to life
than all these
tales of woe

–

He has all the love
the love she has to give
he is the reason
the reason
she needs
needs to live

–

A gun in your hand
finger on the trigger
with hate in your heart
pull the trigger
be a killer

–

Life without you
has little
little value

–

Who wrote my script?
All this shit
must have been dumb
dim, a halfwit

–

Ask the angels

–

She wanted a divorce
because I wasn't hung
hung like a horse
she said don't be crude
don't be coarse

–

Quick on your feet
to survive on the street
sharp of mind
to earn a dime

–

They say
animals and children
can tell
is he from Heaven
Heaven or hell?

–

Don't suffer in silence

–

In a world of your own
playing games
on your,
on your phone

–

I've spent a lifetime
drinking something
might as well be moonshine
or something similar
it tastes and feels
very familiar ...
it's certainly not fine
fine French wine

–

No one speaks when you meet
meet in the street
looks you in the eye
as they pass you by
danger in a stranger

–

Tears of God

–

You're unique
but no freak
you've smiled for
for a while
but no antique

–

Told you once
I won't tell you twice
the man can be cruel
sometimes not very nice
–

For all those who live today
your sacrifice
will never fade
the ultimate price
that you all paid
–

Did they make mankind
one-eyed and blind
who kill and maim
all in a false god's
false god's name
–

Roll back the years
just golden souvenirs
from our yesteryears
–

We speak the same language
seldom disagree
speak for the poor
set them free
–

I've got this energy
energy flowing through me
like electricity
some form of chemistry
–

I'm the lady
Brad Pitt can't resist
the girl he's dying to kiss …
I wish

–

Feed the chickens
the pigs and the horses
feed the ducks
a good old countrywoman
likes a good old country!

–

I was married to a cracker
she left me for a big fat knacker …
now I'd like to thank her
for running off with that
with that wanker.

–

CPSIA information can be obtained
at www.ICGtesting.com
Printed in the USA
BVHW071508121021
618743BV00001B/29